Everyday Prayers for
FAMILIES

D1714264

EVERYDAY PRAYERS FOR FAMILIES

Copyright © 2011 Chris Coe
Material for this book first appeared in:
Prayers for Fathers, by Kevin Mayhew Ltd, Buxhall, England.
Prayers for Mothers, by Kevin Mayhew Ltd, Buxhall, England.
Prayers for Your Baby's Baptism, by Kevin Mayhew Ltd, Buxhall, England.
Prayers for Your Birthday, by Kevin Mayhew Ltd, Buxhall, England.
Prayers for Your Marriage, by Kevin Mayhew Ltd, Buxhall, England.
Prayers for Your New Baby, by Kevin Mayhew Ltd, Buxhall, England.
Footprints and Other Favorite Prayers, by Kevin Mayhew Ltd, Buxhall, England.
My Confirmation Prayer Book, by Kevin Mayhew Ltd, Buxhall, England.
Prayers for a Friend, by Kevin Mayhew Ltd, Buxhall, England.
Prayers for a Gardener, by Kevin Mayhew Ltd, Buxhall, England.

This edition copyright © Augsburg Books 2021 , an imprint of 1517 Media.

Cover image: Chris Coe
Cover design: Emily Wyland

Print ISBN: 978-1-5064-6811-2

Everyday Prayers for
FAMILIES

Chosen and illustrated
by Chris Coe

Augsburg Books

MINNEAPOLIS

Children are God's great gift to the world
and caring for them until they are grown
up is one of the most important tasks that
God gives us. As you read these prayers and
meditations, be thankful and proud to
be doing it.

Remember the perfect example of our
Father in heaven, who is always willing to
guide and encourage, as you cherish and
nurture those entrusted to you. God will help
you to grow daily in love, grace, patience,
and wisdom when you put your faith in him.

A Family Prayer

Dear Father in heaven,
I ask for your touch;
bless all my family,
we need you so much.
Grant us your wisdom
to choose what is right,
to walk in your pathways
of truth and light.
Strengthen our family
with faith to hold fast,
to cherish and nurture
the treasures that last.

Teach us love,
to forgive and to share
in the realms of the spirit,
to thrive and to dare.
But most of all, Lord,
when our journey is through,
bind us together,
forever with you.

Family and Friends

Lord, behold our family here assembled.
We thank you for this place in which we dwell,
for the love that unites us,
for the peace accorded to us this day,
for the hope with which we expect the morrow,
for the health, the work, the food,
and the bright skies that
make our lives delightful;
for our friends in all parts of the earth.

Amen.

Robert Louis Stevenson (1850–1894)

The Lord's Prayer

Our Father who art in heaven,
hallowed be thy name.
Thy kingdom come,
thy will be done,
on earth as it is in heaven.
Give us this day our daily bread;
and forgive us our trespasses,
as we forgive those
who trespass against us.
And lead us not into temptation
but deliver us from evil.
For thine is the kingdom,
the power, and the glory,
forever and ever.

Amen.

The 23rd Psalm

The Lord is my shepherd,
I shall not be in want.
He makes me lie down
in green pastures,
he leads me beside quiet waters,
he restores my soul.
He guides me in paths of righteousness
for his name's sake.
Even though I walk through
the valley of the shadow of death,
I will fear no evil,
for you are with me;
your rod and your staff,
they comfort me.

You prepare a table before me
in the presence of my enemies.
You anoint my head with oil;
my cup overflows.
Surely goodness and love
will follow me
all the days of my life,
and I will dwell
in the house of the Lord
forever.

The Art of Marriage

A good marriage must be created.
In marriage, the little things are the big things.
It is never being too old to hold hands.
It is remembering to say "I love you"
at least once a day.
It is never going to sleep angry.
It is having a mutual sense of
values and common objectives.
It is standing together and facing the world.
It is forming a circle of love that
gathers in the whole family.
It is speaking words of appreciation
and demonstrating gratitude in thoughtful ways.
It is having the capacity to forgive and forget.

It is giving each other an
atmosphere in which each can grow.
It is a common search for the
good and the beautiful.
It is not only marrying the right person.
It is being the right partner.

Lord, help us to remember
when we first met and the strong love
that grew between us;
to work that love into practical things
so nothing can divide us.
We ask for words both kind
and loving, and hearts always
ready to ask for forgiveness
as well as to forgive.
Dear Lord, we put
our marriage into
your hands.

The Lord is my light and my salvation.

Psalm 27:1

And my God will meet all your needs according
to the glorious riches in Christ Jesus.

Philippians 4:19

The Ring

I give you this ring
as a sign of our marriage bond.
I honor you with my body.
I give you all that I am,
and share with you all that I have,
in the love of God the Father,
God the Son,
and God the Holy Spirit.

Amen.

Never will I leave you or forsake you.

Hebrews 13:5

The Marriage Vows

I take you to be
my wedded husband/wife,
for better, for worse,
for richer, for poorer,
in sickness and in health,
to love and to cherish,
from this day forward,
until we are parted by death;
and this is my solemn vow.

Lord, help us to realize
the seriousness of these vows.
We cannot possibly know the future,
but give us the strength and grace
to meet each day as it comes,
with an ever-strengthening love.
May the good things enrich us.
May the bad things
only bring us closer together.
May no sin or foolishness
or human weakness
ever drive us apart.
Hold us every day
in your loving hands.

Amen.

Peter Dainty

Look to the Lord and his strength;
seek his face always.

Psalm 105:4

Husband and Wife

We thank you, Lord,
at the start of our married life.
We thank you for each other
and the love that has
grown between us.
May it go on growing.
And may it be a love
that reaches out
beyond our own two lives,
to embrace our wider families.
May we have a welcoming house,
with a hospitable door
to all who come.

May our circle of friends
never be too exclusive
to include another.
And may our marriage
be blessed with children,
so that in loving them,
we can teach them to love you,
the source of all love.
In such simple ways
may love expand
until it reaches
everywhere.

Peter Dainty

Thank the Lord, for he is good.
His love endures forever.

1 Chronicles 16:34

Marriage Blessing

We thank You, O God, for the love
you have implanted in our hearts.
May it always inspire us to be
kind in our words, considerate of feelings,
and concerned for each other's
needs and wishes.

Help us to be understanding and forgiving
of human weaknesses and failings.

Increase our faith and trust in you and may
your prudence guide our life and love.

Bless our marriage, O God,
with peace and happiness,
and make our love fruitful for your glory
and our joy both here and in eternity.

The Lord has given good things to you.

Deuteronomy 26:11

How great is the love the Father
has lavished on us.

1 John 3:1

And now faith,
hope, and love abide,
these three;
and the greatest of these
is love.

1 Corinthians 13:13

The blessing of the Lord be upon you.

Psalm 129:8

Thank you, God,
for this special friendship
we enjoy.
The laughter and
the tears we share.
The being there
in times of need.
The comfortable contentment
in one another's company.
My blessing is my friend.

Susan Sayers

Peter asked Jesus,
"If someone offends me,
how often should I forgive;
say, seven times?"
Jesus answered,
"Not merely seven times,
I tell you,
but seventy times seven."

Matthew 18:21, 22

In him our hearts rejoice,
for we trust in his holy name.

Psalm 33:21

God has not promised
sun without rain,
joy without sorrow,
peace without pain.
But God has promised
strength for the day,
rest for the laborer,
light for the way,
grace for the trials,
help from above,
unfailing sympathy,
undying love.

Annie Johnson Flint

God Bless You

How sweetly fall those simple
words upon the human heart;
when friends in holiest terms thus
seek their best wish to impart.
From far or near, they ever seem
to bear a power to cheer you;
and soul responsive beats
to soul in breathing out:
"God bless you."

A Promise of Hope

I alone know the plans
I have for you,
plans to bring you prosperity
and not disaster,
plans to bring about
the future you hope for.

Then you will call to me.
You will come and pray to me,
and I will answer you.

You will seek me,
and you will find me
because you will seek me
with all your heart.

Jeremiah 29:11-13

Rejoice in the Lord always.

Philippians 4:4

Know and believe today that the Lord is God.

Deuteronomy 4:39

Lord Jesus,
I do not know what might happen to me, I
do not know where I might have to go, but
I do know you are with me
and you will guide me
on my journey through life.
Lord Jesus, as you seek to be my friend,
let me welcome you each day.

Amen.

David Adam

Christ is with me, Christ is before me,
Christ is behind me, Christ is within me,
Christ is beneath me, Christ is above me,
Christ on my right and on my left.
Christ all around me and within.

Saint Patrick

The Father
watches over you.

The Son our Savior
blesses you.

The Holy Spirit
comes to you.

The very fullness
of our God
becomes your gift,
your guide for life.

Prayer for Patience

When my patience
seems too short,
help me to stretch it;
teach me how to meet
a crisis with a smile.

When I'm running out
of quick and clever answers,
let the questions stop
for just a little while.

When it seems as though
the day has too few hours,
in which to do the things
I have to do,
may I always find the time
for what's important—
time for listening,
time for love,
and laughter, too.

The Lord will watch over your coming and
going both now and forevermore.

Psalm 121:8

Let us be grateful
for the capacity to see, feel, hear,
and understand.
Let us be grateful for
this incredible gift of life.
Let us be especially grateful
for the ties of love that bind us together,
giving dignity, meaning, worth,
and joy to all our days.
This is indeed a day
that the Lord has made.
Let us rejoice in it and be glad,
and let us count our many blessings.

Loving Father,
as we join our bodies in love,
may we share
in your creative power
of joy and fruitfulness.

Jesus, Son of God,
as you gave yourself
in love for all the world,
help us to give ourselves
in love to each other.

Holy Spirit of God,
bind us together
with a bond of love
that cannot be broken.

Amen.

Peter Dainty

The Lord your God will be
with you wherever you go.

Joshua 1:9

May the Lord make your love for each
other increase and overflow.

1 Thessalonians 3:12

May the Lord bless you and keep you.

Numbers 6:24

Be at Peace

Do not look forward
to what might happen tomorrow;
the same everlasting Father
who cares for you today
will take care of you
tomorrow and everyday.
Be at peace, then, and put aside
all anxious thoughts and imaginings.

Francis de Sales

If I Could

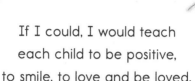

If I could, I would teach
each child to be positive,
to smile, to love and be loved.

I would teach each child to take time
to observe some miracle of nature—
the song of a bird,
the beauty of a snowflake,
the orange glow of a winter sunset.

I would teach each child to feel warmly
about those for whom the task of learning
does not come easily.

I would teach each one to be kind
to all living creatures
and to crowd out of their lives
feelings of guilt, misunderstanding,
and lack of compassion.

I would teach each child that it is alright
to show their feelings by laughing,
crying, or touching someone they care about.

Every day I would have a child feel special
and through my actions,
each one would know how much
I really care.

May you be blessed by the Lord,
the Maker of heaven and earth.

Psalm 115:15

Ask God to bless each child
and guide them in their life.
Thank God for them
and place them in
God's care.

Susan Sayers

Caring for little ones
until they are grown up
is one of the most important
jobs God gives us.
Be proud to be doing it,
and thankful.

Susan Sayers

He gathers the lambs in his arms
and carries them close to his heart.

Isaiah 40:11

I will make the darkness light and the
rough ground smooth.

Isaiah 42:16

An Everyday Prayer

Lord, in all I do today,
remind me that
there's just one way
to do things
that I do best,
to put my mind
and heart at rest.
And that's to put
in your great hands,
my life, that you alone
have planned.

We bless you, Lord,
for the beauty of the trees,
the softness of the air,
the fragrance of the grass.

We bless you, Lord,
for the soaring of the skies,
the rhythms of the earth,
the stillness of the night.

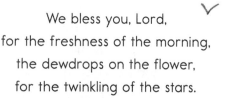

We bless you, Lord,
for the freshness of the morning,
the dewdrops on the flower,
for the twinkling of the stars.

We bless you, Lord,
for the taste of good food,
the trail of the sun,
and the life that never goes away.

Chief Dan George

God said, "See, I have given you
every plant yielding seed
that is upon the face of all the earth,
and every tree with seed in its fruit;
you shall have them for food.
And to every beast of the earth,
and to every bird of the air,
and to everything that creeps on the earth,
everything that has the breath of life,
I have given every green plant for food."
And it was so.
God saw everything that he had made,
and indeed, it was very good.

Genesis 1:29-31

I will put my trust in him.

Hebrews 2:13

Children, obey your parents in the Lord,
for this is right.
"Honor your father and mother"—
which is the first commandment
with a promise—
"that it may go well with you and that
you may enjoy long life on the earth."
Fathers, do not exasperate your children;
instead, bring them up in the training
and instruction of the Lord.

Ephesians 6:1-4

In all your ways acknowledge him,
and he will direct your paths.

Proverbs 3:6

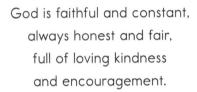

God is faithful and constant,
always honest and fair,
full of loving kindness
and encouragement.

It's a good model for parents
and caregivers to follow!

Susan Sayers

You won't get it right
all of the time.
But God will help you
do your best
and then look after
the rest.

Susan Sayers

For everything there is a season,
and a time for every activity under heaven.

Ecclesiastes 3:1

God Makes
the Difference

In all of our days,
so many wonderful,
beautiful ways,
the blessings he sends
from his own loving hand,
are better than anything
we could have planned.

His love for his children
is daily expressed;
like a father he gives
nothing less than his best.

His gifts and his goodness
fill life to the brim,
with a joy that could only
be fashioned by him.

Lord God, we thank you
for the great gift you give
the world, in children.

Give us grace to dedicate ourselves
to one another and to you,
to be channels to each other
of your priceless love,
freely given and freely received.

Jesus took the children
in his arms and blessed them.

Mark 10:16

This is the day that the Lord has made;
let us rejoice and be glad.

Psalm 118:24

Don't tell your children
to say their prayers,
but pray with them
as they go to bed,
thanking God together
for the day.

Susan Sayers

When I sleep and when
I wake thank you, Lord, for being there,
a constant companion,
daily strength,
and faithful friend.

Nick Fawcett

The God of peace will be with you.

Philippians 4:9

Mary's Slumber Song

O child of hope, what shadows fall
across your sleeping eyes:
shadows of a future
marked by love and sacrifice?
O child of promise, such a cost,
but such a prize!
O softly slumber,
child of grace!

Child of sorrow, child of joy,
child of mystery divine,
may your peaceful, trusting sleep
be of hope the seal and sign.
O softly slumber,
child of grace!

Michael Forster

Mother Earth

Dear mother earth, who day by day
unfolds rich blessing on our way,
O praise God! Alleluia!
The fruits and flowers that verdant grow,
let them his praise abundant show.
O praise God, O praise God,
Alleluia! Alleluia! Alleluia!

St. Francis of Assisi

Thank you, O God,
for the wonderful gift of a child.
Hold us together in your love,
and in the community
of your people.
As we grow together,
may we be signs of
your grace to one another.

The Lord has done this,
and it is marvelous in our eyes.

Psalm 118:23

God has poured out his love into our hearts.

Romans 5:5

Love Is Patient

Love is patient and kind;
it is not jealous
or conceited or proud;

Love is not ill-mannered
or selfish or irritable;
love does not keep
a record of wrongs.

Love is not happy with evil,
but is happy with the truth.

Love never gives up;
and its faith, hope,
and patience never fail.

1 Corinthians 13:4-7

The joy of the Lord is your strength.

Nehemiah 8:10

Kitchen Prayer

Lord of pots and pans and things,
since I've not time to be
a saint by doing lovely things,
or watching late with thee,
or dreaming in the dawn light,
or storming heaven's gates,
make me a saint by getting meals
and washing up the plates.
Although I must have
Martha's hands,
I have a Mary mind,
and when I shine the boots and shoes,
thy sandals, Lord, I find.
I think of how they trod the earth,
each time I scrub the floor;
accept this meditation, Lord,
I haven't time for more.

Cast your burden on the Lord
and he will sustain you.

Psalm 55:22

Every work of love
brings a person
face to face
with God.

Mother Teresa

Let me hear joy and gladness.

Psalm 51:8

The Lord will guide you always.

Isaiah 58:11

A Gaelic Blessing

May the road rise up
to meet you,
may the wind be always
at your back.
May the sun shine warm
upon your face,
the rain fall soft
upon your fields
and until we meet again,
may God hold you
in the palm of
his hand.

Don't Quit

When things go wrong as they sometimes will;
when the road you're trudging seems all
uphill; when funds are low and debts are high
and when you want to smile but you have to
sigh; when care is pressing you down a bit,

rest, if you must, but don't you quit.
Life is strange with its twists and turns
as every one of us sometimes learns,
and many a failure turns about when
they might have won had they stuck it out.
Don't give up though the pace seems slow,
and you may succeed with another blow.

Success is failure turned inside out,
God's hidden gift in the clouds of doubt. You
never can tell how close you are,
it may be near when it seems so far.
So stick to the fight when you're hardest hit.
It's when things seem worst
that you must not quit.

You shall go out in joy and be led forth in peace.

Isaiah 55:12

Lord, bless our family
with openness,
with sharing in all
our joys and sorrow,
with freedom to let
each other grow,
with understanding
and with love,
no matter what,
no matter where.

The Lord gives strength to his people.

Psalm 29:11

Solomon's Wisdom

God, you gave me a child,
originally part of me,
initially dependent on me,
given to me to love,
to nurture,
and to set free.

Not mine to possess,
but mine to love;
not mine to own,
but mine to respect;
not mine to grasp at,
but mine to hold.

God give me Solomon's wisdom,
to recognize true love
in the willingness to let go.

Michael Forster

Children are a gift from the Lord.

Psalm 127:3

May mercy, peace, and love
be yours in abundance.

Jude verse 2

May God,
who understands each need,
who listens to every prayer,
bless me and keep me
in his loving, tender care.

Never forget
God's great love for you,
knowing you are loved
will make you smile more.

You are not there
to drive the children forward
but to enable them to grow.

Susan Sayers

I am with you and will watch over you
wherever you go.

Genesis 28:15

I have loved you with an everlasting love.

Jeremiah 31:3

Lord you are my shepherd,
my protector, and my guardian.
You have given your life eternal.
You will lead me into the way of peace
if only I will follow you.
I thank you for your love
and sacrifice for me.

Amen.

David Adam

May the Lord bless you
and take care of you.
May the Lord be kind
and gracious to you.
May the Lord look on you
with favor and give you peace.

Numbers 6:24-26

The Lord is my strength and my song.

Exodus 15:2

Lord Jesus, you are my King.
Come and rule in my heart
that your kingdom may come in me.
Lord, I give thanks to you
for you are my Savior.

Amen.

David Adam

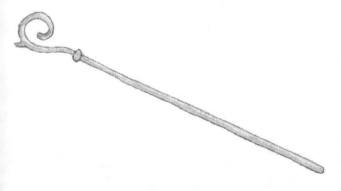

Growing up

How difficult it seems
to watch our children grow up!
They start to think for themselves,
make their own mistakes,
as well as repeating ours.
Sometimes, we don't understand them.
Sometimes, they don't understand us.
They bring us pain,
they bring us joy.
Either way, we want to cling,
keep them close to us.

Happy Birthday

May God richly bless you
on your birthday
as once again
we celebrate with thankfulness
the precious gift of your life.
May the light of God
surround you always.
And may you hear
the quiet whisper
of God's love
along the way.

Susan Sayers

Let everything that has breath praise the Lord.

Psalm 150:6

You are a child
of the living universe,
fed by stored sunshine
from the nearest star.

You are unique and beautiful,
cherished by God.

Susan Sayers

God bless this baby,
newly born, with all the
gentle love of heaven.
A miracle, wrapped up
and fast asleep,
reminding us again
of human hope
and innocence.

Susan Sayers

He will love you and bless you.

Deuteronomy 7:13

I said a prayer for you today
and know God must have heard—
I felt the answer in my heart
although he spoke no word!

I didn't ask for wealth or fame
(I knew you wouldn't mind)—
I asked him to send treasures
of a far more lasting kind!

I asked that he'd be near you
at the start of each new day
to grant you health and blessings
and friends to share your way!

I asked for happiness for you
in all things great and small—
but it was for his loving care
I prayed the most of all!

 Frank J. Zamboni

Great is the Lord and most worthy of praise.

Psalm 96:4

Heavenly Father, give this child
a deep love of learning,
and the wisdom to understand
how to use the knowledge s/he gains.
May s/he know the joy of curiosity
and wonder in your beautiful world.
May s/he never stop asking questions.

Lord of all, bless this child
with a deep sense of joy and happiness
throughout their life.
When times are hard—
as sometimes they will be—
may s/he still have a thankful heart
for blessings received,
and for your faithful presence.

Susan Hardwick

Sing to the Lord all the earth.

Psalm 96:1

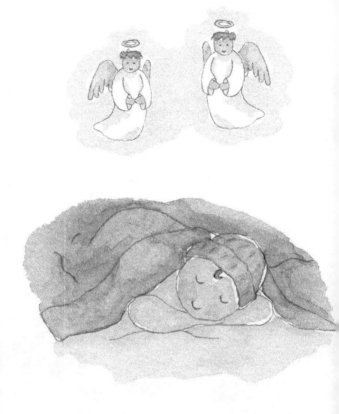

The Lord blesses his people with peace.

Psalm 29:11

Lord Jesus Christ, our Lord most dear,
as you were once an infant here,
so give this child of yours, we pray,
your grace and blessing day by day.

Their watch let angels round her/him keep
where'er s/he be, awake, asleep.
Be pleased your caring love to give,
and keep this child by morn and eve.

Heinrich von Laufenberg (15th Century)
trans. Catherine Winkworth (1827-78)

Jesus is pleased to come to us
as the truth to be told
and the life to be lived,
as the light to be lighted
and the love to be loved,
as the joy to be given
and the peace to be spread.

Mother Teresa

It fell upon a summer day,
when Jesus walked in Galilee,
the mothers from the village brought
their children to his knee.

He took them in his arms, and laid
his hands on each remembered head.
"Suffer these little ones to come
to me," he gently said.

"Forbid them not. Unless you bear
the childlike heart your hearts within,
unto my kingdom you may come,
but may not enter in."

Then, Jesus, look upon this child
that he may come to you and feel
your hands on him in blessing laid,
love-giving, strong to heal.

Stopford Augustus Brooke (1832-1916)

He has given us great and precious promises.

2 Peter 1:4

May you grow in strength, little one,
and use your strength for good.
May you grow in knowledge, little one,
and temper it with wisdom.
May you grow in faith, little one,
and learn to trust in God.
May you grow in love, little one,
and walk in it all your days.

Peter Dainty

Give thanks to the Lord!

Psalm 105:1

He gives rain on the earth and sends
waters on the fields.

Job 5:10

Twinkle, twinkle little star,
how I wonder what you are.
God made you
and God made me,
made the moon
and sky and sea.
Twinkle, twinkle little star,
how I wonder what you are.

Susan Sayers

Sing and make music in your heart.

Ephesians 5:19

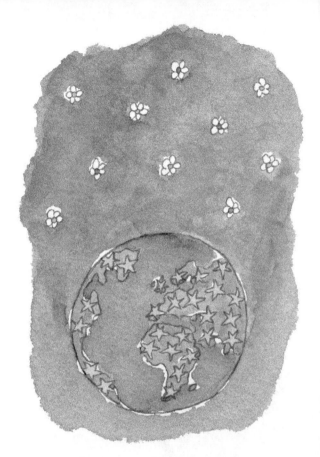

Praise him, sun and moon;
praise him, all you shining stars!

Psalm 148:3

Precious one,
so small,
so sweet;

dancing in
on angel feet;
straight from
heaven's brightest star;

what a miracle
you are.

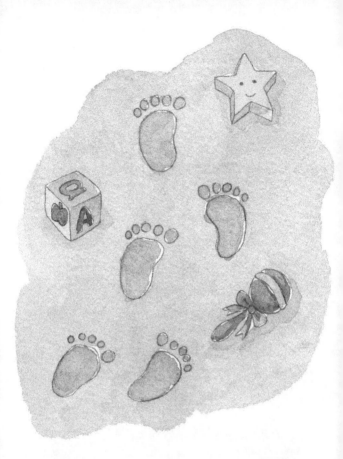

Lord you have done such great things.

Psalm 92:5

Every good and perfect gift
is from above,
coming down from the
Father of heavenly lights,
who does not change like
shifting shadows.

James 1:17

Almighty God
and heavenly Father,
we thank you for the children
which you have given to us.
Give us grace to bring them up
in your faith, reverence, and love,
that as they advance in years,
they may grow in grace,
and be found in the number
of your own family;
through Jesus Christ our Lord.

John Cosin (1596-1672)

The Lord is good.
His love continues forever.

Psalm 100:5

May the whole earth be filled with his glory.

Psalm 72:19

And there were shepherds
living out in the fields near by,
keeping watch over their flocks at night.
An angel of the Lord appeared to them,
and the glory of the Lord
shone around them,
and they were terrified.
But the angel said to them,
"Do not be afraid. I bring you good news
of great joy that will be for all the people.
Today in the town of David
a Savior has been born to you;
he is Christ the Lord.
This will be a sign to you:
you will find a baby wrapped in cloths
and lying in a manger."

Luke 2:8-12

I know the plans I have for you,
says the Lord.

Jeremiah 29:11

Heavenly Father,
we thank you from our hearts
for our new baby
whom you have sent into our lives
and put into our care.
We ask for grace and wisdom
as we take on the responsibility
for this new life.
May our child grow
in strength and understanding,
and learn the joy
of walking in your ways,
through Jesus Christ our Lord.

Amen.

I will praise you, O Lord, with all my heart.

Psalm 138:1

May the Lord bless you
and take care of you.
May the Lord be kind
and gracious to you.
May the Lord look on you
with favor and give you peace.

Numbers 6:24-26

I have called you by name
and you are mine.

Isaiah 43:1

Whoever welcomes one of these little children
in my name welcomes me.

Mark 9:37

There's a miracle
called Friendship
that dwells within the heart
and you don't know
how it happens
or when it gets its start.
But the happiness
it brings to you
always gives a special lift
and you realize
that friendship
is God's most precious gift.

The Baby's Prayer

Though I may be very small
and all around me big and tall,
Abba, Father, you are near,
so I have no need to fear.

Though I have no words to say,
you will teach me day to day.
There are thoughts within my mind,
which sense what's good
and know who's kind.

As I sleep, and play, and feed,
you remind me what I need:
just one word from heaven above,
and that word is simply—love.

Amen.

Peter Dainty

Blessed are the pure in heart.

Matthew 5:8

I am the good shepherd.

John 10:11

See Israel's gentle Shepherd stand
with all-engaging charms.
Hark how he calls the tender lambs,
and folds them in his arms.

"Permit them to approach," he cries,
"nor scorn their humble name.
For 'twas to bless such souls as these
the Lord of angels came."

We bring them, Lord, in thankful hands,
and yield them up to thee.
Joyful that we ourselves are thine,
thine let our children be.

Philip Doddridge (1702–51)

You did not choose me, but I chose you.

John 15:16

I will give them joy in my house of prayer.

Isaiah 56:7

"Let the children come to me;
do not stop them;
for it is to such as these
that the kingdom of God belongs.
Truly I tell you, whoever does not
receive the kingdom of God
as a little child will never enter it."
And he took them up in his arms,
laid his hands on them,
and blessed them.

Mark 10:14-16 (NRSV)

As for me and my family, we will serve the Lord.

Joshua 24:15

Heavenly Father, we thank you
that you welcome little children
into your family,
just as Jesus welcomed them
by holding them in his arms
and blessing them at his knee.
We thank you that you love them
before they even know you,
or can even speak your name.
Help us to show them your love
by being loving and patient
toward them ourselves,
and telling them of Jesus,
who gave himself in love
for all the world.

Amen.

Peter Dainty

May the Lord watch over you
and give you peace.

Numbers 6:26

May you know
length of life
and sun-filled days,
and may you not
have to depart this life
before your own child
falls in love.

Traditional Irish blessing

A friend is like a tower strong;
a friend is like a joyous song
that helps us on our way.

When golden ties of friendship bind
the heart to heart, the mind to mind,
how fortunate are we!

For friendship is a noble thing;
it soars past death on angel's wing
into eternity.

God blesses friendship's holy bond
both here and in the great beyond:
a benefit unpriced.

Then may we know that wondrous joy,
that precious ore without alloy:
a friendship based on Christ.

When you're lonely,
I wish you love.

When you're down,
I wish you joy.

When you're troubled,
I wish you peace.

When things are complicated,
I wish you simple beauty.

When things look empty,
I wish you hope.

From this day on
may the truth
of God's word
grow strong
in your heart
and may
the gentle love
of Jesus
fill your life
now and
always.

Life-giver,
bring buds to flower,
bring rain to the earth,
bring songs to our hearts.

Renewer,
may gardens become green,
may beauty emerge,
may dreams come to pass.

Friends are the flowers in the garden of life.
They help you through times of trouble and strife.

There's nothing like friends to make a heart sing.
True friends will share with you most everything.

They will not abandon you in times of need.
They aren't overcome by envy or greed.

Friends are the icing on life's great cake.
Real friends will give and allow you to take.

I don't know how I would survive without friends.
They applaud my beginnings and mourn my sad ends.

Tell me, please tell me, what I would do,
if I didn't have a garden full of friends just like YOU!

And the peace of God, which transcends
all understanding will guard your hearts
and minds in Christ Jesus.

Philippians 4:7

May our loving
heavenly Father
guide and keep me
in his care.
May the blessings
of the Holy Spirit
all be mine to share.
May God's wisdom
be the light that leads
my footsteps every day
and his presence
my companion
as I walk along life's way.

Go therefore
and make disciples
of all nations,
baptizing them
in the name of the Father
and the Son
and of the Holy Spirit.

Matthew 28:19

The Cross in My Pocket

I carry a cross in my pocket,
a simple reminder to me
of the fact that I am a Christian,
no matter where I may be.
This little cross is not magic,
nor is it a good luck charm,
it isn't meant to protect me
from every physical harm.
It's not for identification
for all the world to see,
it's simply an understanding
between my Savior and me.

When I put my hand in my pocket
to bring out a coin or key,
the cross is there to remind me
of the price he paid for me.
It reminds me, too, to be thankful
for my blessings day by day
and strive to serve him better
in all that I do and say.
It's also a daily reminder
of the peace and comfort I share
with all who know my master
and give themselves to his care.

So I carry a cross in my pocket,
reminding no one but me
that Jesus Christ is Lord of my life
if only I'll let him be.

Verna Mae Thomas

The Lord will go with you.
He will not forget you.

Deuteronomy 31:6

Prayer of Dedication

Lord Jesus,
I give you my hands to do your work.
I give you my feet to go your way.
I give you my eyes to see as you do.
I give you my tongue to speak your words.
I give you my mind that you may think in me.

I give you my spirit that you may pray in me.
Above all, I give you my heart
that you may love in me.
I give you my whole self
that you may grow in me,
so that it is you, Lord Jesus,
who lives and works and prays in me.